Contents

Chapter 1
The human heart

The human heart performs an incredible job. Every day, it pumps blood around the body through a network of tubes called **blood vessels**. As it does so it makes sure that **oxygen** reaches the **organs**, which allows them to work. It also ensures that waste from the body is carried away. The heart is the powerhouse of the entire human body.

The heart is the size of a grapefruit and it is located almost in the centre of the chest, between the lungs. You can feel your heartbeat when you place your hand on the left side of your chest. This is because the heart is angled a little and a part of it taps against the left side of the chest as it beats. The heart is a vital organ. It is protected by the rib cage, the bones that form the chest.

When you exercise, your heart pumps blood to your muscles.

The HEART

Richard and Louise Spilsbury

Raintree is an imprint of Capstone Global Library Limited, a company incorporated in England and Wales having its registered office at 264 Banbury Road, Oxford, OX2 7DY – Registered company number: 6695582

www.raintree.co.uk
myorders@raintree.co.uk

Produced for Raintree by Calcium
Editors: Sarah Eason and Harriet McGregor
Designers: Paul Myerscough and Simon Borrough
Picture researcher: Rachel Bloun
Originated by Capstone Global Library Limited © 2018

ISBN 978 1 4747 6580 0 (hardback)
22 21 20 19 18
10 9 8 7 6 5 4 3 2 1

ISBN 978 1 4747 6595 4 (paperback)
23 22 21 20 19
10 9 8 7 6 5 4 3 2 1

British Library Cataloguing in Publication Data
A full catalogue record for this book is available from the British Library.

Acknowledgements
Cover art: Shutterstock: Denk Creative.
Picture credits: Shutterstock: Atm2003 12b, Tewan Banditrukkanka 36, Blend Images 4–5, BlueRingMedia 16, Busayamol 8–9, Gianni Caito 40–41, Designua 7r, Elenabsl 19, Fabiodevilla 34–35, Firma V 28–29, Juan Gaertner 26b, Garsya 8l, Imtmphoto 6–7, Dmitry Kalinovsky 32–33, Sebastian Kaulitzki 5, 21, 29br, Khuruzero 36–37, Lightspring 1, 15r, Magnia 30–31, Negovura 42–43, NoPainNoGain 10–11, Oculo 33r, Oorka 24–25, Lisa S. 34b, Ljupco Smokovski 14–15, Stihii 13, Syda Productions 26–27, John T Takai 39, Tefi 20, Wouter Tolenaars 18–19, Udra11 44bl, Vectorstockstoker 22, Vetpathologist 24l, Tom Wang 44–45.

Every effort has been made to contact copyright holders of material reproduced in this book. Any omissions will be rectified in subsequent printings if notice is given to the publisher.

All the internet addresses (URLs) given in this book were valid at the time of going to press. However, due to the dynamic nature of the internet, some addresses may have changed, or sites may have changed or ceased to exist since publication. While the author and publisher regret any inconvenience this may cause readers, no responsibility for any such changes can be accepted by either the author or the publisher.

Printed and bound in China.

The heart must beat every minute of every day to keep the body alive. The walls of the heart are made of a special type of muscle called cardiac muscle. Unlike skeletal muscles, which pull on your bones to make body parts such as your arms and legs move, cardiac muscle does not get tired, even though it works all the time. It circulates the blood around the body three times every minute.

Get smart!

Blood goes on an epic journey as it is pumped through the human body. There are 100,000 kilometres (61,137 miles) of blood vessels in your body. If you laid them end-to-end, they would travel all the way around the world twice!

Blood vessels carry blood to and from the heart.

Parts of the heart

The heart is usually described as a pump, but really it is like two pumps side by side. The heart is divided into two halves. Each half is divided into two blood-filled areas called chambers.

Each of the two chambers that make up the upper part of the heart is called an atrium. Together they are called the **atria**. The heart has a left atrium and a right atrium. The two chambers that form the lower part of the heart are called the left and right **ventricles**. There is also a thick layer of muscle called the septum running down the middle of the heart. It separates the left side and right side of the heart.

First, the atria chambers fill with blood. They push that blood into the ventricles. Next, the ventricles pump the blood out of the heart. At the same time as the ventricles squeeze the blood out of the heart, the atria refill with blood. **Valves** between the chambers stop blood moving the wrong way.

Doctors listen to the heart using a stethoscope.

Valves open up to let blood move from one chamber to another and close again to stop the blood flowing backwards. The mitral valve and the tricuspid valve let blood flow from the atria to the ventricles. The aortic valve and pulmonary valve control the flow of blood leaving the heart.

Get smart!

The distinctive "lub-dub, lub-dub" sound of a heart is caused by the heart valves closing. The lub sound happens when the mitral and tricuspid valves close. The next dub sound happens when the aortic and pulmonary valves close after the blood has been squeezed out of the heart.

The atria and ventricles of the heart work together to keep blood circulating.

right atrium

pulmonary valve

tricuspid valve

left atrium

mitral valve

aortic valve

left ventricle

right ventricle

In a heartbeat

The heart beats more than once every second, about 100,000 times every single day and about 35 million times in a year. During an average human lifetime, a human heart beats more than 2.5 billion times. The human heart is one of the most hard-working organs in the body.

The heart beats (pumps) by contracting, which is another word for tightening or squeezing. After the atria have filled with blood, the cardiac muscles contract to squirt the blood along. If you squeeze your hand into a fist, release, and then squeeze again you will get an idea of how the heart chambers contract to squirt out the blood. This is also about the same amount of force the heart muscles use to work. The difference is that the heart does this every second, even while you are resting or sleeping.

To measure how fast a heart beats people take their pulse rate. You can feel your pulse by lightly pressing two fingers on pulse points. These are the places you can see large blood vessels called **arteries** just beneath the skin. You should be able to feel a small throb beneath your fingers. This is the pulse, and it is caused by the contractions of your heart creating waves of **pressure** along the arteries.

The walls of the heart squeeze its chambers to squeeze out blood, similar to squeezing toothpaste out of a tube.

Take your pulse rate by resting your fingers on the side of your neck. Count the number of beats in 1 minute.

Get smart!

A child's average heart, or pulse, rate when sitting is 90–to 120 beats per minute. As an adult, the pulse rate slows to an average of 72 beats per minute, when resting.

Get flow chart smart!

A heartbeat

This flow chart shows what happens when a heart beats.

Blood enters the atria chambers of the heart.

The aortic and pulmonary valves close so the blood cannot flow back again.

The atria contract, or squeeze, to force blood through valves into the ventricle chambers.

Once the blood has passed through, the mitral and tricuspid valves close. This stops blood flowing back into the atria.

The left and right ventricles contract and force the aortic and pulmonary valves open to squeeze blood out of the heart.

Flowchart Smart

The movement of the blood through the heart and around the body through an intricate network of blood vessels is called the circulatory system. The heart is so efficient that it takes less than 1 minute to pump blood to every part of the body.

The blood in the circulatory system is on a loop. Blood enters the right side of the heart through large blood vessels, called the venae cavae. Then it is pumped through pulmonary arteries to the lungs. As the blood passes through the lungs it collects oxygen, which the body has breathed in from the air outside. Then this oxygen-rich blood is pumped back through the pulmonary **veins** to the left side of the heart.

The heart then pumps the blood out through the aorta, the biggest artery in the body. The blood vessels that carry blood away from the heart are called arteries. They are the thickest blood vessels in the body because the pressure on the blood vessels is strongest at this point, when blood leaves the heart. The walls of the arteries contain muscles that contract (squeeze and tighten) to keep the blood moving away from the heart.

The aorta, the largest artery in the body, is about the width of a garden hose.

As well as pumping blood to other parts of the body, the heart needs a supply of blood to work itself. Coronary arteries supply blood to the heart. There are two coronary arteries that branch off from the aorta near the point at which the aorta and the left ventricle meet. These arteries divide into a network of smaller blood vessels that provide oxygen and nourishment to the heart muscles.

The blood vessels that carry blood back to the heart are called veins.

13

Into the cells

After leaving the heart, oxygen-rich blood travels through the arteries and into smaller blood vessels called arterioles. From there it travels into blood vessels called **capillaries**. Capillaries are so narrow that ten of them equal the thickness of a human hair. Even though they are tiny, capillaries are a very important part of the circulatory system. They deliver blood to the **cells**.

Get smart!

Oxygen and **digested** food passes from the capillaries into cells by **diffusion**. Diffusion is when a substance moves from a region where it is in high concentration to a region where it is in low concentration. Capillaries have very thin walls, so substances pass quickly and easily from them into cells. A huge length of capillaries surround and pass close to each cell, so there is a large **surface area** through which oxygen and dissolved food can pass.

Oxygen-rich blood travels around the body to help muscles work during exercise.

Cells make up all the different parts of the body. These red and white blood cells make up part of the blood along with plasma and **platelets**.

Capillaries reach individual cells so the bloodstream can deliver oxygen to them. Digested food from the **digestive system** is carried in the blood **plasma**. This also passes from the capillaries into the cells. The cells use oxygen to release **energy** from glucose, a type of sugar, in the dissolved food so they can live, work and grow.

Capillaries connect the arteries with the veins. After delivering oxygen and dissolved food to the cells, blood moves back through capillaries to larger blood vessels called venules. Then it enters larger veins until it reaches the venae cavae and returns to the heart and lungs to collect fresh supplies of oxygen.

Get flow chart smart!

Blood flow around the body

Let's look at how the heart pumps blood around the body once more, using a flow chart.

Blood is drawn into the right side of the heart.

Blood is pumped out of the right side of the heart through arteries to the lungs.

In the lungs, blood collects oxygen. It's then pumped back to the left side of the heart.

The heart pumps this oxygen-rich blood through the main artery, the aorta.

Blood travels all the way around the body.

Flowchart Smart

Chapter 3
Waste disposal

We can think of the blood travelling from the heart as a fleet of delivery lorries carrying oxygen and food to the cells. When the cells combine oxygen with glucose to release energy, they make waste that must be removed. The bloodstream carrying the waste away from the cells is a little like the body's bin lorry!

When we exhale on a cold day we can see the water form droplets in the air.

When people combine fuel and oxygen to make electrical energy in a power plant, the waste that comes out of the power plant chimney is **carbon dioxide**, a type of gas. **Respiration** is the process in which cells combine oxygen and glucose to release energy, water and waste substances such as carbon dioxide. Carbon dioxide can be poisonous if it builds up inside the body, so the cells must remove it.

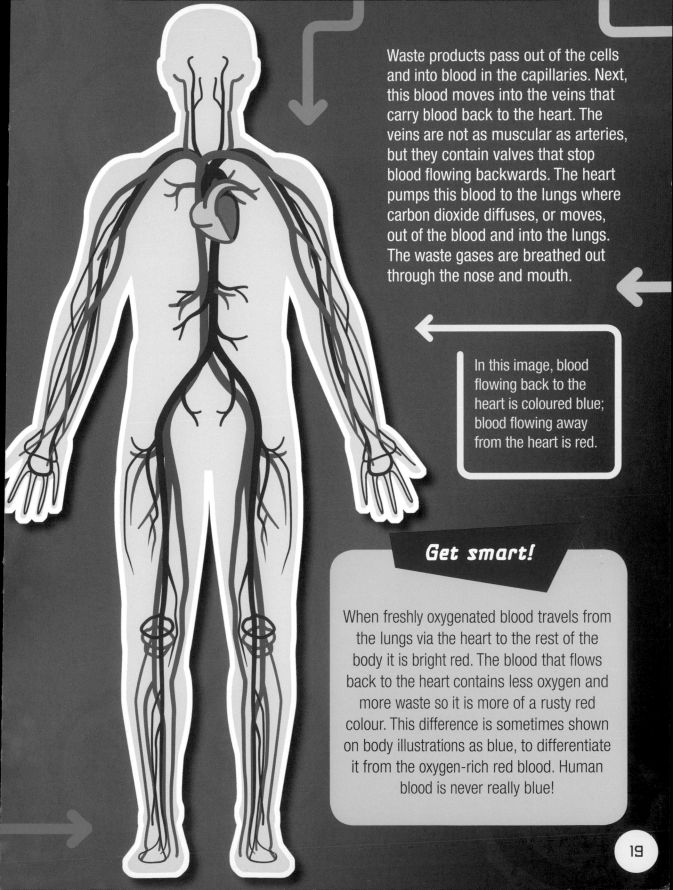

Waste products pass out of the cells and into blood in the capillaries. Next, this blood moves into the veins that carry blood back to the heart. The veins are not as muscular as arteries, but they contain valves that stop blood flowing backwards. The heart pumps this blood to the lungs where carbon dioxide diffuses, or moves, out of the blood and into the lungs. The waste gases are breathed out through the nose and mouth.

In this image, blood flowing back to the heart is coloured blue; blood flowing away from the heart is red.

Get smart!

When freshly oxygenated blood travels from the lungs via the heart to the rest of the body it is bright red. The blood that flows back to the heart contains less oxygen and more waste so it is more of a rusty red colour. This difference is sometimes shown on body illustrations as blue, to differentiate it from the oxygen-rich red blood. Human blood is never really blue!

Through the kidneys

As blood circulates through the blood vessels it also passes through the kidneys. The kidneys are two bean-shaped organs located just below the rib cage, one on each side of the backbone. Each kidney is roughly the size of an adult fist. The kidneys are important because they remove waste and excess (extra) fluid from the blood to keep it clean and healthy.

Each kidney consists of about one million filtering units called **nephrons**, so small they can only be seen with a high-powered microscope. Each nephron has a filter, called the glomerulus, and a tubule. The glomerulus allows fluid and waste products to pass through it, but not blood cells. The filtered fluid then moves through the tubule, which removes wastes from it and then sends any useful products, such as minerals, back to the blood. Some of the waste that the kidneys filter out of the blood, such as excess water, comes from cell processes. Some waste is substances that your body does not need because it already has enough of them, such as proteins.

The kidneys make urine from the excess fluid, waste and other unwanted substances they filter from the blood. Urine flows down through narrow tubes called ureters to the bladder where it is stored. Then the urine is passed out of the body through a tube called the urethra.

The kidneys are so important to our health that we have two of them, so we can survive if one gets injured or stops working.

The kidneys filter the blood up to 400 times a day. They filter 114-142 litres (120-150 quarts) of blood to produce 1-2 litres (1-2 quarts) of urine, which consists of wastes and excess fluid.

Get flow chart smart!

The kidneys are protected from injury by a large padding of fat, the lower ribs and several muscles.

Waste removal

This flow chart explains how the circulatory system removes waste from the body's cells.

During respiration, cells use oxygen and glucose to release energy. This creates carbon dioxide as waste.

The carbon dioxide passes up the throat and is exhaled through the nose and mouth.

The heart pumps the blood to the lungs where carbon dioxide diffuses out of the blood.

Carbon dioxide passes out of the cell and into the blood in the capillaries.

This blood contains little oxygen and some waste. It is now rusty red instead of bright red.

The blood travels from capillaries to veins and back to the heart.

Flowchart

Smart

Chapter 4
Blood

An average adult has about 5.6 litres (6 quarts) of blood in their body. Blood is mostly made up of yellowish fluid called plasma. This is the liquid part of the blood and it contains a lot of water. The plasma carries the other three most important parts of the blood: red blood cells, white blood cells and platelets.

One drop of blood contains about five million red blood cells.

New blood cells are made in the **bone marrow**, the soft sponge-like material found in the centre of some bones.

Red blood cells are the most common type of blood cell. They are shaped like slightly squashed, flattened discs. They contain a substance called **haemoglobin**, which is what makes red blood cells look bright red. Each **molecule** of haemoglobin is made up of four iron **atoms**. These are important because they capture oxygen molecules as blood passes through the lungs. They release the oxygen as the blood travels around the body. Each red blood cell only lives for about four months, but the body is constantly making new blood cells to replace those that wear out.

Most red and white blood cells are made by stem cells in the **bone marrow**. A baby's body has blood-cell producing bone marrow in all their bones. As people get older, the marrow in many bones stops working. As adults, blood cells are made in bones such as the ribs, parts of the humerus (upper arm bone) and femur (thigh bone).

Get smart!

Everyone's blood belongs to one of four different groups, which are known by the letters: A, B, AB and O. Each of the four different blood types can also either be "Rhesus positive" or "Rhesus negative" depending on whether or not it has a certain molecule on its cells. Do you know what blood type you have?

White blood cells

There are fewer white blood cells in the blood than red blood cells, but they do a very important job. White blood cells defend the body against **infection** and stop us getting harmful diseases. When the body fights an infection, it can make more white blood cells to battle the disease.

There are several types of white blood cells with different jobs. For example, imagine someone digs in soil without wearing gloves. Then they eat their lunch without washing their hands. Bacteria from the ground enter their mouth and get into their bloodstream. Some of these bacteria can cause infections and disease. Lymphocytes are white blood cells that identify bacteria and other harmful body invaders, which we call antigens. The lymphocytes release special proteins called **antibodies**, which stick to the antigens.

When the antigens are labelled with antibodies, other white blood cells such as granulocytes can find and destroy them. After the white blood cells have learned to recognize and destroy a particular infection, lymphocytes will quickly attack the same bacteria if it enters the body again.

These lymphocytes are attacking a cancer cell.

The body makes more white blood cells when someone is ill, to help them fight the infection.

Get smart!

When yellow pus seeps from an infected wound, it looks pale because it is mostly made up of white blood cells. These are white blood cells that have worn themselves out defending the body against infection. White blood cells live from a few days to several months. Like red blood cells, they are constantly being replaced.

Blood clots

When the skin is cut or damaged, blood leaks from the body's blood vessels. Blood loss is dangerous, so the body immediately works to close the gap. Platelets are like the blood's repair kit. They group together at wounds, helping the blood to clot (set) and repair damaged blood vessels. Platelets are tiny oval-shaped cells. When a blood vessel breaks, platelets gather in the area and form a plug that stops the leak. They seal the wound by sticking both to the wound and to each other. They produce a stringy substance called fibrin. The fibrin forms a web that traps water and cells to form a clot.

Get smart!

Anaemia is a condition in which someone has fewer healthy red blood cells than normal. Anaemia can be caused by blood loss or a lack of iron in the diet, and by certain diseases such as leukaemia. People who are anaemic may feel weak and tired and they may look paler than they usually do.

After platelets plug small leaks and stop or slow the bleeding, other clotting factors create a strong, stable clot. Clotting factors are proteins in the blood that control bleeding. Many different clotting factors work together to stop bleeding and form solid lumps to seal leaks, wounds, cuts and scratches. This can occur inside and on the surface of the body. If a large blood vessel is cut, platelets and clotting factors may not be able to repair it. Instead a doctor uses stitches and dressings to control the bleeding.

Fibrin strands are made of protein and are very tough. They trap cells to form a clot.

This wound has been stitched to keep it closed. You can see where the clots of blood have dried and begun to harden into a scab.

Get flow chart smart!

Blood vessel repair

Follow the steps to see how blood heals damaged blood vessels.

When a person cuts him or herself, blood leaks from broken blood vessels.

Platelets in the blood flow to the wound and collect there to plug the gap. They release fibrin to stop more blood escaping.

The clot hardens into a scab. This is a crusty covering that stops more dirt and bacteria entering the blood.

Clotting factors in the blood create a strong, stable clot and control the bleeding.

White blood cells attack bacteria entering the blood through the cut.

Flowchart Smart

Chapter 5
Heart and circulation problems

The first known person to have died from heart disease was a princess in ancient Egypt who died 3,500 years ago. Scientists have used modern scanning equipment to study her mummified body and have discovered she had blocked arteries, a common problem today.

Sometimes people with blocked arteries need surgery to unblock them. Surgeons must re-route blood through other blood vessels to bypass the blockage.

Blocked coronary arteries cause heart attacks. A heart attack happens when the blood supply to the heart muscles is interrupted. The coronary artery supplies blood to the heart, and blockages form when fatty deposits build up inside it, restricting the flow of blood to the heart. Without fresh supplies of oxygen and fuel, the heart muscles cannot work. A heart attack can happen when a blood clot forms on the fatty deposits in the artery, or if a piece of the deposit breaks away and plugs the space inside the artery.

Circulation problems happen when deposits build up in other blood vessels, too. The deposits narrow veins and capillaries and lead to poor circulation in other body parts such as fingers and toes, or internal parts such as the digestive system. In mild cases it can just cause a little discomfort. If it worsens, however, it can affect vital organs and be very serious.

healthy artery

narrowed artery

blocked artery

Get smart!

Have you ever sat awkwardly with your legs crossed for a long time until it feels like the limb has fallen asleep? By putting pressure on **nerves** and blood vessels you have prevented messages and blood flow from reaching the leg. The good news is that it soon returns to normal once you change position and the pressure is off.

Blood matters

When the body has a small wound or cut, blood clots and the body repairs itself. If someone is in a major accident and loses a lot of blood, they will need a blood transfusion.

A transfusion is when a patient is given blood from a blood donor, someone who has donated their blood. It is vitally important that the correct type of blood is given to a patient and that the blood has been checked to be sure it does not contain any infections. If donated blood is infected in any way at all, it is destroyed. Donated blood is also tested for blood type to make sure it is compatible with the recipient's blood type.

People must only receive transfusions of the same type of blood as their own. This is because there are tiny **antigens** on the surface of the red blood cells. These antigens are proteins and sugars that the body uses to recognize other blood cells in the body. If blood containing "foreign" antigens enters the body, the patient's blood will reject the new blood. This is life threatening. Great care is taken by medical professionals to make sure this does not happen.

Giving blood doesn't hurt, and it only takes the donor's body about two weeks to make new blood to replace that which they donated.

A blood transfusion can save a person's life if they experience sudden, heavy blood loss in an accident.

Get smart!

When people donate blood, it can be separated into its different parts. This is so that people can not only receive whole-blood transfusions, but they can also be given transfusions of one of the parts of their blood that they lack, such as platelets, plasma or red blood cells.

Helping the heart

The study of the human heart and its disorders is known as cardiology. Cardiologists are doctors who use different machines to examine the human heart and help people with heart problems.

Electrical impulses make muscle cells contract and cause the heart to beat. An electrocardiogram (ECG) is a machine that measures the electricity in a patient's heart. Sensors attached to the skin detect the electrical signals produced by the heart each time it beats. It shows the signals as a line moving across a screen that occasionally spikes (shoots upwards). Cardiologists use information collected by the ECG to find out if a patient is having heart rhythm problems or even a heart attack.

TIME	NIBP	NIBPm	HR	SpO2	RR	T1
13:30:34	132/87	96	101	---	18	--.-
13: :	158/100	112	109	---	23	--.-
13: :33	145/89	100	101	---	16	--.-

The green line is the read-out from the ECG machine. An ECG is a quick, safe and painless test.

A pacemaker is a life-saving machine that helps people with a weak or irregular heartbeat. A pacemaker is a small, battery-powered unit that is implanted inside a patient's body. Wires, called electrodes, are attached to the heart from this unit. The pacemaker delivers electrical pulses, which work like tiny electric shocks, and make the heart muscles contract and beat regularly again.

Get smart!

Amazingly, in a few cases where someone has a very badly diseased heart, doctors carry out a heart transplant operation. They replace a failing heart with a healthy heart from a donor who has recently died. It is a risky operation that is only carried out on someone whose life is at great risk because their heart no longer works effectively.

Get flow chart smart!

How a pacemaker works

In this flow chart see how a pacemaker keeps a person's heart beating regularly.

A pacemaker is implanted inside a patient's body, just above the rib cage.

The electrical pulses work like tiny electric shocks and make the heart muscles contract and beat regularly again.

Wires, called electrodes, connect the heart to the pacemaker.

The pacemaker delivers regular electrical pulses to the heart.

Flowchart

Smart

Chapter 6

Taking care of your heart

To keep the body's heart and circulatory system healthy, people need regular exercise, a balanced diet and medical care if any problems arise.

The heart is a muscle and, like any muscle, it must be exercised to become strong. Cardiovascular exercise such as swimming, dancing or playing football makes you breathe harder and faster. When you exercise like this or run around a lot, your muscles need a lot more oxygen-filled blood.

To cope with the extra demands of exercise, the body temporarily directs blood flow away from areas that do not need it as much, such as the digestive system, and sends it towards the muscles instead. This increases the blood flow and therefore the amount of blood returning to the heart at any one time. When people exercise regularly, the left ventricle of the heart becomes bigger so it is ready to hold and release more blood at once. When each heartbeat delivers a bigger burst of blood, the heart does not have to contract quite as often. This reduces the amount of work it does and is why cardiovascular exercise helps your heart stay stronger for longer.

Tennis is a great sport for strengthening your heart.

Get smart!

When you run, you may have noticed feeling your heart pounding in your chest. That is because it is working harder. Try taking your pulse before and after a short period of exercise. What do you notice? Try to be active and get your heart working harder for at least 30 minutes every day if you can.

Get flow chart smart!

Exercise and the heart

This flow chart is a reminder of how exercise helps the heart.

A person runs around and begins to breathe harder and faster.

The muscles use the extra oxygen from the increased blood supply to make more energy.

As they take in more oxygen, there is more oxygen-filled blood circulating around the body and entering the muscles.

The body directs blood flow away from areas that do not need it as much and sends it towards the muscles.

Flowchart

Smart

Play it safe

Eating a balanced, healthy diet is good for the whole body, including the heart and circulatory system. A healthy diet also helps prevent problems such as blocked arteries and heart disease.

Foods that contain a lot of fat, such as burgers, chips, crisps, chocolate and cake, should be eaten only occasionally. These fatty foods can lead to clogged arteries.

Medical professionals recommend eating at least five servings of fruit and vegetables each day, and wholemeal bread, brown rice, wholewheat pasta, fish and lean meat to help keep arteries clear. Smoking damages the heart and blood vessels, too. It damages the lining of the arteries, leading to a build-up of fatty material, which narrows the blood vessels and can increase the risk of a heart attack.

A balanced diet includes fruit, vegetables and grains.

When we eat more food than our body requires to make the energy it needs, the excess is stored as fat. These stores of fat can be used to release energy when the body needs it. The problem is that if people regularly eat more than they use, these fat stores build up and people become overweight. Being overweight puts a strain on the heart and can cause other health problems too.

The heart is an incredibly hard-working organ and the body's circulatory system is vital for our health and survival. Remember, the heart does more work than any other muscle in the body, so we should do all we can to take care of it, so it can go on looking after us!

Activity is fun, burns energy and keeps your heart healthy.

Glossary

antibodies substances produced by the body to fight disease

antigens substances that the body does not recognize and so tries to destroy

arteries blood vessels that carry blood away from the heart to the capillaries

atoms smallest particles of a substance that can exist by themselves

atria upper chambers of the heart where blood collects before passing to the ventricles

blood vessels tubes that carry blood around the body

bone marrow substance inside bones that makes new blood cells

capillaries tiny blood vessels that connect the arteries and veins

carbon dioxide gas in the air

cells very small parts that together form all living things

diffusion when a substance moves from a region where it is in high concentration to a region where it is in low concentration

digested broken down so the body can use it

digestive system body parts that together break down food we eat so the body can use it

energy capacity to do work

haemoglobin protein that transports oxygen in the blood

infection disease caused by bacteria that enter the body

molecule tiny particle of a substance made from two or more atoms

nephrons tiny filtering structures in the two kidneys

nerves fibres that carry messages between the brain and the rest of the body

organs body parts such as the heart or liver

oxygen gas in the air

plasma colourless fluid part of blood

platelets tiny cell fragments in blood that help stop bleeding when the body is injured

pressure pushing force

respiration process by which the body takes in oxygen and uses it to release energy from food

surface area total area of the surface of a 3-D object

valves flaps that close to keep blood from flowing in the wrong direction

veins blood vessels that carry blood from the capillaries to the heart

ventricles two main chambers of the heart: left and right